DESOLATION

same mirror different reflection different same mirror
same mirror different reflection same mirror
different reflection different mirror different refl
same reflection different mirror different r
different reflection different mirror differe
different same mirror different reflection diffe
different same reflection different mirror dif
different same mirror different reflection
different same reflection different mirror reflect
different same mirror different same refl
different same reflection different mi
different same mirror different r
different same reflection differe
different same mirror diffe
different same reflection di
different same mirror
different same reflectio
different same
different reflec
different sam
different s
differer
differ
dif

same mirror different reflection same mirror

DESOLATION

frankie baby

Long Day Press
Chicago

Copyright © 2024 frankie baby

Published by Long Day Press
Chicago, Il 60647
LongDayPress.com
@LongDayPress

All rights reserved. This is a work of fiction. No part of this book may be reproduced for any reason or by any means without written permission excepting brief passages for reviewing or educational purposes, provided the Author and Publisher are acknowledged in the reproduction. Why would you steal from us?

ISBN 978-1-950987-45-0 (Paperback Edition)
ISBN 979-8-8691-5336-4 (eBook Edition)
Library of Congress Control Number: 2024930847

Edited by Joshua Bohnsack

Printed in the United States of America.
First Edition

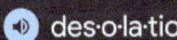

Dictionary
Definitions from Oxford Languages · Learn more

🔊 **des·o·la·tion**
/ˌdezəˈlāSH(ə)n/

noun

a state of complete emptiness or destruction.
"the stony desolation of the desert"

Similar: barrenness   bleakness   starkness   bareness   dismalness   grimness   ⌄

- anguished misery or loneliness.
"in choked desolation, she watched him leave"

Similar: misery   sadness   unhappiness   melancholy   gloom   gloominess   ⌄

BABY'S RECORD

NAME _Mogilewski, Girl_

Birthdate _1-2-89_ Sex _Female_

Mother's Name _Kataryne_

Address _____

Birth weight _7-2_

Discharge weight _7-0_ Date _1/3/89_

length _19"_

head circumference _13.5"_

Baby's data:

Apgar score - 1 minute _9_ 5 min _10_
Blood type _O+_ Coombs test _neg_
Cord Serology _DR_
Peak bilirubin _____ mg.% Date _____
Hematocrit _____ date _____

Prenatal history:
Problems _none_

Delivery:
☐ c/s   ☒ vaginal
Problems _____

Physical Exam:
☒ Normal
☐ Problems _Nevus flammeus_

Metabolic screen _1/3/89_ date _____

Repeat screen _____ date _____

i was born from the body of a woman i have never met

13

the worst gift i have ever received is life

what they don't tell you about being adopted

you are a stranger inside your own body
you will hate your body before you see it for the first time

you will hate families who look alike

you will hate identical twins

nothing has permanence

people disappear

abandoment is real

you will wonder
you will wonder who she was and why she did it

you will tell yourself things

you won't care
you will care

you will wonder if she died
and if she tried to find you

you will care so much it will drive you toward
insanity at 100mph
you will crash into the divider
you will burn alive in the wreckage of not knowing

15

broken nose
bleeding rose

in kindergarten i hated my classroom
there was a sandbox inside of it
f i l t h
sand in their pockets
in their hair
wet noses
like pigs in shit

for my 6th birthday i didn't want a party. i wanted to be left alone. i wanted a cake. i wanted donuts. i wanted lip smackers chapstick. i wore them on a string. around my neck. when my mom asked me why i didn't want to invite anyone over. i said i can't trust that i'll be friends with them forever. to have them in the photos would ruin them. people who disappear don't deserve a party. or cake. or donuts.

i hated soccer.

i refused to play. i sat down on the side of the field during games. picking the grass out. one by one. plucking them from their life source. making a pile. the game was over. i did not celebrate wins or losses. i did not attempt to make friends. i did not see the fun in team sports. i did enjoy the pizza and gatorade.

> i hated ballet and tap and jazz
> i had no desire
> to dance

i did not want to perform for others

piano lessons - i was gifted
'she really just gets it'
i refused to let anyone hear me play
my talents are my own

18

in the water
i am weightless
i am invisible
i am alone

                        swim
but it never felt like a team
      overheard phrases
      i didn't understand
         exotic
          tan

you. dont. look. like   darker
  anyone

19

in the water

there is no air left

in my lungs

i push myself   as fast as possible

i am close to death

not

when i was 9 my parents went bankrupt and got a divorce. not because of the money. because they hated one another. i stayed with my mom. i don't think i had a choice. i remember hiding in the laundry room. in the dark. sitting on the washing machine. if they can't find me. i don't have to go.

for an entire summer i stayed inside. i had no friends. i didn't know anybody. i watched tv. i ate whatever was around. and then i ate more. i found comfort in food. i found control. no one could stop me. no one was there to. you cannot fill a void with food.

when i was 11 my mother took me to a nutritionist because she thought i was fat. the nutritionist agreed. in her weird white office, with ugly grey carpeting, the nutritionist handed me a weird glob. a yellowing gelatinous thing. i looked down at it. i squeezed it hard. it felt like it was oozing through my fingers. but it was sturdy. it was imprinted with the number one. she told me that's what 1 pound of fat looked like. she told me that's what my body was full of. she said if i get hungry i can have a pickle.

now when I go out to dinner i ask for no pickles on my burger. i do not ever want anyone else's pickle. i do not want to smell a pickle. i do not want to see a pickle. the pickle is my enemy.

21

when i was 12 a girl named mary called me fat.
i punched her in the face and got suspended
nobody called me fat again
not to my face

i ate more
never in front of anyone else

when i was 13 my neighbors sister moved to texas for college. one night she was returning a movie to blockbuster. when she left the parking lot two men followed her jeep in their car. they ran her off the road. they kidnapped her and murdered her.
that's when my fear of texas was started

when i was 14 my mother sent me to fat camp but they called it weight loss camp. it was an 8 week program. it was sleep away camp. on the first day they had weigh-in. one by one we went to the auditorium. there was a scale on the stage. the audience was empty except for a few staff members. one by one we had to walk across the stage and stand on the scale. the number behind us on a large screen, so the staff could see. they told us what we weighed. one woman said i wasn't really fat enough for this camp but i was kinda fat in comparison to normal kids.

mtv true life: i'm going to fat camp filmed that summer. they only wanted really fat kids on camera. i wasn't fat enough for mtv.

the camp had a swim team. i joined because it meant i could stay in the pool for most of the summer. there were swim meets. we would go to other nearby sleep away camps and compete. at one of the regular non-fat camps the other kids called us fat.
to them — i was fat enough

23

allowed

*limit the fruit

- watermelon
- romaine
- cucumbers
- chicken broth
- turkey
- diet snapple
- eggs
- carrots
- rice cakes
- broccoli
- grapefruit
- chicken
- kale
- decaf tea
- coffee (black)
- spinach
- apples
- oatmeal
- popcorn (plain)
- water
- celery
- diet coke
- splenda
- diet soda
- skim milk
- lean cuisines

not allowed

- bagels
- french fries
- cookies
- hot dogs
- pasta
- slushies
- butter
- mozzarella sticks
- soda
- french toast
- mayo
- onion rings
- cereal
- ice cream
- pancakes
- bread
- nachos
- rice
- cake
- bacon
- cheeseburgers
- waffles
- pizza
- alfredo sauce
- burritos
- cream cheese

24

summer camp
eating disorders   body dysmorphia
lanyard keychains   tie-dye
fat free ice cream   plain popcorn

                 i lost more than weight
                    i lost my worth

25

when i was 15 i went to applebee's with my mom. i ordered an asian chicken salad. with a diet coke. i now know that salad isn't healthy and neither is diet soda. she told me when we get home she had something to show me. i wanted to know then and there. tell me now i asked. she said she had my original birth certificate and a photocopy of my birth mother's passport. i can still remember the face i made. i could make it again right now if someone asked me to. my left eyebrow lifted. my eye twitched. what do you mean you have it? and you waited this many years to tell me this? she said she didn't think i wanted to see it.

we drove home in silence

when we got there i no longer wanted to see it.

i still have not seen it

sometimes for a split second it feels like i can

so i do

27

coffee
keys
wallett

coconut
tanning
soda

phone
gum
gloss

mask
mask
sanitizer

book
edibles
lotion

silent
first
time

sour
spoiled
rotten

diet snapple
newports
pills

train
delay
i was skinny   always

28

self-sabotage
i've never known true love
real love
i couldn't understand why
someone wanted to be with me
being adopted is a curse
at first
i couldn't believe he wanted
me
i was scared
he would leave
at any given moment
he could go   i did the only thing i knew how
i was not worth staying for   i ate
                                to fill the void
                                that could not be filled
                                with food
                                or anything else
                                but answers
                                empty
                                trying to make myself
                                full

i ate and ate and ate
    and he still loved me
        he did not leave

                                           but i still couldn't trust his existence

29

when i was 17 and 10 months my mother convinced a doctor that the only way i would ever be happy was if i was permanently thin and the only way to ensure that was by having gastric bypass surgery

i was slightly under 200lbs

when i was 18 years and 5 days old i had gastric bypass surgery

one year later

i was slightly under 100lbs

my mother told me i was too skinny

30

what they don't tell you about gastric bypass is that you absorb things differently. alcohol goes right to your bloodstream. pills hit you almost immediately. tolerance

before
      i

knew
    it
      i

        was   before
      addicted   i
                    knew

                    it

                the
                  girl

              i
                  was

n o   l o n g e r   e x i s t e d

31

at 21
my mother tricked me
into rehab

                                    at 23 i was out

at 24 i had to start over

       again

when i was 25
i donated my kidney
if someone wanted to live that badly
they deserved it

i am jealous of blue eyes

                i am jealous of people who feel nothing

       i am jealous of people who wear t-shirts

              i am jealous of people
              who know who they are

i am jealous of people who look like their parents

i am jealous of people who are happy
       inside their body

              i am jealous of people who can eat

i am jealous of people who can still get high

              i am jealous of people who feel everything

34

nothing worth noting happened from 26-28
    i wanted to be boring
    i wanted to just exist

        i got bored

28 was the year of the relapse
        i was drunk everyday
    everynight

    slurring through the east village

    when you are on the edge of a cliff
you are the most alive

35

got sober (again)
at 30

misery soon followed

someone on a tv show said the end is just the beginning and i thought it was the dumbest fucking thing i have ever heard

then i started to wonder about her again

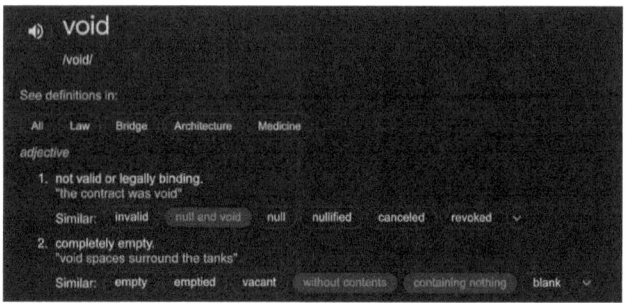

as if i don't already know
the result of my search
for

myself

37

23 and me sat on my desk for two years

i watched the death toll
go up
up
up
the streets of brooklyn
silent
wailing
of the ambulance
they pass my window
every 7 minutes
knowing
the person inside   months later
won't make it   down dekalb
another day   i hear the chants
                        i hear the screams
                        black lives matter
                             i hear
                           the sounds
                               of
                     people fighting to live
                            yet again

when will i find my will to live

losing weight. i look too skinny. i feel too fat. ca
hungry. food is unappealing. i am gaining weigh
eight. i look too skinny. i feel too fat. can't eat. i am
od is unappealing. i am gaining weight. i am losing
skinny. i feel too fat. can't eat. i am never hungry.
ng. i am gaining weight. i am losing weight. i can't e
ngry. food is unappealing. i am gaining weight. i an
ook too skinny. i feel too fat. can't eat. i am never h
ppealing. i am gaining weight. i am losing weight. i
el too fat. can't eat. i am never hungry. food is una
g weight. i am losing weight. i look too skinny. i fee
m never hungry. food is unappealing. i am gainin
weight. i look too skinny. i feel too fat. can't eat. i a
od is unappealing. i am gaining weight. i am losing
skinny. i feel too fat. can't eat. i am never hungry.
ng. i am gaining weight. i am losing weight. i look to
at. can't eat. i am never hungry. food is unappeali
eight. i can't eat. i am never hungry. food is unapp
g weight. i am losing weight. i look too skinny. i fee
m never hungry. food is unappealing. i am gainin
weight. i look too skinny. i feel too fat. can't eat. i a
od is unappealing. i am gaining weight. i am losing
weight. i look too skinny. i feel too fat. can't eat. i a
od is unappealing. i am gaining weight. i am losing
skinny. i feel too fat. can't eat. i am never hungry.
ng. i am gaining weight. i am losing weight. i look to
at. can't eat. i am never hungry. food is unappeali
eight. i am losing weight. i look too skinny. i feel too
never hungry. food is unappealing. i am gaining w
am never hungry. food is unappealing. i am gainin
g weight. i look too skinny. i feel too fat. can't eat. i a
od is unappealing. i am gaining weight. i am losing
skinny. i feel too fat. can't eat. i am never hungry.
ling. i am gaining weight. i am losing weight. i can't e
ngry. food is unappealing. i am gaining weight. i an

there's something about knowing
after an entire life of not
that makes me uncomfortable
i thrive in the secrecy
of self
no one can know me
if i do not know myself
the email unread
months pass me by
i cower   i cave
the results were
a n t i c l i m a c t i c
my father / 50% indian
my mother / 50% eastern european
i am evenly
the product of
two strangers
i don't care about my father
different than the way
i don't care about
my mother
because when i say i dont care
about my mother
i   a m   l y i n g

men

                      go blameless

i only have more questions
i have less of an idea of myself
there was before
and after
i'm in the after
lying to myself about the beginning
imagination can keep you sane

1. It causes insanity in the adoptee. It causes traumatic separation anxiety at birth, which affects the entire nervous system. Next, it develops into a Post Traumatic Stress Disorder (PTSD). And because it takes so long for an adoptee to realize the true causes of their anxiety and depression... adoptees realize this at 30 years of age by then it's almost too late.

14. Because it is me against the world. The pain never goes away.

17. It left me with a hole inside and searching for faces in crowds.

19. Because I don't trust people or allow them to love me.

37. I hate adoption because it prohibits me from having answers.

38. It deprives me of my full identity.

42. I hate adoption because it is bittersweet.

39. It conceals the truth.

```
                    same mirror - same reflection - same mirror
          different reflection - different mirror - different reflection
          different reflection - different mirror - different reflection
          different reflection - different mirror - different reflection
          different reflection - different mirror - different reflection
          different reflection - different mirror - different reflection
          different reflection - different mirror - different reflection
            different reflection - different mirror - different
              different reflection - different mirror - differe
                different reflection - different mirror - diffe
                  different reflection - different mirror - di
                   different reflection - different mirror
                    different reflection - different mirro
                     different reflection - different mi
                      different reflection - different
                       different reflection - differ
        same face       different reflection - diffe
   i've seen this hoe    different reflection - diff
       before             different reflection - d
    different face         different reflection
i do not recognize this person  different reflec
       anymore              different reflec
                              different refle
                               different refl
                                different ref
                                 different
                                  differer
                                   diffe
                                    di
```

wya?

omw to heaven
u down?

i wonder
what she would have named me

eastern european girl names

46

alina basha celina
nadia daria juliya

kamila zena kasia truda elga
irina

lada dorota ela karolyna
annika zaria verina ula
darva
micheleka vera halina
radilla ava
wioletta valeska
galina roksana zarya
kataryne

helenka
karlinka maja helenka
felka yelina saskia
pamela karli
zorina

dannika ola zivka olenna
vlada yuliya zosia toshka
sabina mila chesna

vladislava veronika ivanna eva
evgenia pola
monika
marina milanka lyudmila anka

47

nothing fits.

mother.

i'm sorry   i'm drowning

in my   daydreams

are lucid

are lifelike

what is your life like

i wonder

i waver

in your absence
  i feel l o s t

    and f o u n d memories

f l o a t i n g around memories

these are not my memories

i must have made you up

unsure if you're alive

m y fears f l o a t inside

hot air balloons carry so much

weight

i've put some on

is that genetic

i will never know   you

like rain slashing through a window

there is a flood of pain
that i cannot stop

i would like it very much if someone would close it

CLEAN UP MY BRAIN

with a mop

drip   drop

your reflection in the water

your face is s l u r r y   b l u r r y

hurry   up
to your old tricks

the doctor must have said

when you walked into his office

to get rid of another kid

acknowledgments

for laura cronk, for creating an assignment that bloomed into this book

for dylan owens, the first to read and suffer through the sadness of this book... for helping me believe in myself enough to share my desolation with the world

for my mom(s)

for better or worse

frankie baby is a poet from brooklyn.

Long Day Press

New & Forthcoming Titles

In Between My Bodies
Emily Capers
Essays
ISBN: 9781950987467 • $14

Sex With My Family
Jessica Anne
Fictions
ISBN: 9781950987306 • $14

Memory Field
Eric Tyler Benick
Travels
ISBN: 9781950987443 • $16

How to Adjust to the Dark
Rebecca van Laer
Novella
ISBN: 9781950987207 • $16

LongDayPress.com   @LongDayPress

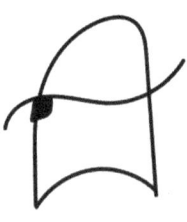

same mirror different reflection same mirror
same mirror different reflection different reflect
same mirror same reflection same mir
different mirror different reflection different refl
different reflection different mirror different reflection same m
different reflection same mirror different reflection same
different reflection same mirror different reflection differ
different reflection same mirror different reflection diffe
different reflection same mirror different reflection dif
different reflection same mirror different reflection
different reflection same mirror different reflec
different reflection same mirror different refl
different reflection same mirror different ref
different reflection same mirror different r
different reflection same mirror differen
different reflection same mirror differe
different reflection same mirror diffe
different reflection same mirror di
different reflection same mirror
different reflection same mir
different reflection same m
different reflection same
different reflec sam
different reflec
different re
different s
differer
differ
dif

different reflection of different mirror or different reflection of same mirror or same reflection of different mirror

www.ingramcontent.com/pod-product-compliance
Lightning Source LLC
Chambersburg PA
CBHW040252090526
44586CB00041B/2811